From

_____

Date

_____

Message

_____

_____

_____

30
Days to Becoming a Woman of Prayer
BOOK OF PRAYERS

Stormie Omartian

HARVEST HOUSE PUBLISHERS
EUGENE, OREGON

Cover by Garborg Design Works, Savage, Minnesota

Cover photo © Bigstock / Luna Vandoorne

Back cover author photo © Michael Gomez Photography

30 DAYS TO BECOMING A WOMAN OF PRAYER BOOK OF PRAYERS
Previously published as *The Power of a Praying® Life Book of Prayers*
Copyright © 2010 by Stormie Omartian
Published by Harvest House Publishers
Eugene, Oregon 97408
www.harvesthousepublishers.com

ISBN 978-0-7369-5364-1(pbk.)
ISBN 978-0-7369-5363-4 (eBook)

Printed in the United States of America

21 / VP-NI / 10 9 8 7 6

Introduction

IN ORDER TO HAVE a close walk with God, we
need to pray. A lot! About everything! Having a close
relationship with God only happens if we are praying
every day and making an effort to keep His Word in
our heart. When we do this consistently, we can find
the freedom, wholeness, and true success God has for
us. It is what we need to do in order to see our life
work well. This little book of prayers was designed
to help you with all that.

The prayers in this book are part of the longer prayers found in my book *30 Days to Becoming a Woman of
Prayer*. I have realized—along with countless others—
that having prayers ready to pray as we go about our day
is very helpful in fulfilling our desire to pray more. These
prayers will be a handy reminder to pray about things
you might not have otherwise thought of in your busy

day. They can be an end in themselves or a starting point to more extensive prayer. In any case, they will help you to keep your life on track.

It is *my* prayer for *you* that as you pray, God will speak to your heart about things that are relevant to your life and give you revelation through His Word. Space is provided below each prayer and Scripture for you to jot down these important thoughts.

I know God will bless you every time you are with Him.

Stormie Omartian

Ask, and it will be given to you; seek, and you will find; knock, and it will be opened to you. For everyone who asks receives, and he who seeks finds, and to him who knocks it will be opened.

Luke 11:9-10

1

Know Who Your Father Is

HEAVENLY FATHER, I thank You that You have given me the right to become Your child (John 1:12). Help me to live in Your love and comprehend the depth of Your care and concern for me. Take away any barrier that keeps me from fully understanding what it means to trust You as my heavenly Father. Help me to take on a family resemblance so that I have Your eyes, Your heart, and Your mind. Lord, show me any way in which I need to forgive my earthly father. Heal anything in my heart that has caused me to see You through his failings. Forgive me if I have judged Your perfection by his imperfections. Show me what I need to see, and help me to completely forgive.

*As many as received Him, to them He gave
the right to become children of God, to
those who believe in His name.*

John 1:12

PRAYER NOTES

_____

_____

_____

_____

_____

_____

Know Who Your Father Is

THANK YOU, FATHER GOD, that when I need hope, You are my *Hope* (Psalm 71:5). When I am weak, You are my *Strength* (Isaiah 12:2). When I am weary, You are my *Resting Place* (Jeremiah 50:6). When I need freedom, You are my *Deliverer* (Psalm 70:5). When I want guidance, You are my *Counselor* (Psalm 16:7). When I need healing, You are my *Healer* (Malachi 4:2). When I seek protection, You are my *Shield* (Psalm 33:20). When I am going through a difficult time, You are my *Stronghold in the Day of Trouble* (Nahum 1:7). I am privileged and glad to receive all You have promised Your children. Thank You for being my heavenly Father and the answer to my every need.

Behold what manner of love
the Father has bestowed on us,
that we should be called children of God!

1 John 3:1

Prayer Notes

_____

_____

_____

_____

_____

_____

Receive All Jesus Died for You to Have

LORD JESUS, I know You came "to seek and to save that which was lost" (Luke 19:10). Thank You that You saw my lost condition and have saved me for Yourself and Your purposes. Thank You that because You died for me, I have eternal life and your blood cleanses me from all sin (1 John 1:7). Now I can live free of guilt and condemnation. I believe "there is no other name under heaven" by which I could ever be saved (Acts 4:12). Thank You, Jesus, that I am a joint heir with You of all our Father God's blessings. Thank You for reconciling me to Yourself (2 Corinthians 5:18).

*We have seen and testify that the Father
has sent the Son as Savior of the world.
Whoever confesses that Jesus is the Son of
God, God abides in him, and he in God.*

1 JOHN 4:14-15

PRAYER NOTES

Receive All Jesus Died for You to Have

LORD, thank You that I have the Holy Spirit within me and am no longer controlled by my flesh. Thank You that I have access to a life of hope, healing, power, love, freedom, fulfillment, and purpose. Help me to understand all that You accomplished on the cross. Enable me to live like the new creation You have made me to be. Help me to see my life from Your perspective. Teach me how to receive all that You died to give me. Now, whatever I do in word or deed, help me to do all in Your name, Lord Jesus, giving thanks to God the Father through You (Colossians 3:17).

*If Christ is in you, the body is dead
because of sin, but the Spirit is
life because of righteousness.*

ROMANS 8:10

PRAYER NOTES

Welcome the Holy Spirit's Presence

LORD, in Your presence everything makes sense. When I am with You, I feel Your peace, love, and joy rise in me. When I have not spent enough time with You, I greatly miss that priceless sense of the fullness of Your presence. I come before You and ask You to fill me afresh with Your Holy Spirit today. Cleanse me with Your living water. Wash away anything in my heart of doubt, fear, or worry. Take away everything in me that is not of You. Enable me to walk in the Spirit and not the flesh, and exhibit the fruit of Your Spirit (Galatians 5:16-17). Do a complete work in me so that I can show Your pure love to others.

As many as are led by the Spirit of God, these are sons of God. For you did not receive the spirit of bondage again to fear, but you received the Spirit of adoption by whom we cry out, "Abba, Father." The Spirit Himself bears witness with our spirit that we are children of God.

ROMANS 8:14-16

PRAYER NOTES

Welcome the Holy Spirit's Presence

LORD, teach me everything I need to know about You. Enable me to exhibit faithfulness, gentleness, and self-control (Galatians 5:22-23). You are the Spirit of wisdom, grace, holiness, and life. You are the Spirit of counsel, might, and knowledge (Isaiah 11:2). Spirit of truth, help me to know the truth in all things. Thank You for leading and guiding me. Thank You for being my Helper and Comforter. Thank You that Your Spirit within me enables me to walk in Your ways and do Your commands (Ezekiel 36:27). Help me to pray powerfully and worship You in a way that is pleasing to You. Thank You that You will raise me up to be with You when my life on earth has ended. Until then, lead me ever closer to You.

I will pray the Father, and He will give you another Helper, that He may abide with you forever—the Spirit of truth, whom the world cannot receive, because it neither sees Him nor knows Him; but you know Him, for He dwells with you and will be in you.

JOHN 14:16-17

PRAYER NOTES

_____

_____

_____

_____

_____

Take God at His Word

LORD, I am grateful for Your Word. It shows me how to live, and I realize my life only works if I'm living Your way. Meet me there in the pages and teach me what I need to know. "Open my eyes, that I may see wondrous things from Your law" (Psalm 119:18). Thank You for the comfort, healing, deliverance, and peace Your Word brings me. It is food for my starving soul. Help me to read it every day so that I have a solid understanding of who You are, who You made me to be, and how I am to live. May Your words live in me so that when I pray, I will see answers to my prayers (John 15:7).

*I will worship toward Your holy temple, and
praise Your name, for Your lovingkindness
and Your truth; for You have magnified
Your word above all Your name.*

PSALM 138:2

PRAYER NOTES

_____

_____

_____

_____

_____

_____

Take God at His Word

LORD, my delight is not in the counsel of the ungodly, but it is in Your law. Help me to meditate on Your Word every day and night so that I can be like a tree planted by a river that brings forth fruit and doesn't wither, so that whatever I do will prosper (Psalm 1:1-3). Enable me to live Your way so that my prayers are always pleasing in Your sight (Proverbs 28:9). Your Word reveals what is in my heart. I pray You will cleanse my heart of all evil and expose anything that is not Your will for my life. Teach me the right way to live so that my life will work the way You intend for it to do.

*The word of God is living and powerful, and
sharper than any two-edged sword, piercing
even to the division of soul and spirit, and
of joints and marrow, and is a discerner
of the thoughts and intents of the heart.*

HEBREWS 4:12

PRAYER NOTES

Make Worship a Habit

LORD, I enter Your gates with thanksgiving, and Your courts with praise (Psalm 100:4). I worship You as the almighty, all-powerful God of heaven and earth, and the Creator of all things. No one is greater than You. I praise You as my heavenly Father, who is with me every day to guide and protect me. Thank You for all You have given me, and all You will provide for me in the future. "You guard all that is mine. The land You have given me is a pleasant land" (Psalm 16:5-6 NLT). I praise You for Your love that liberates me and makes me whole. Pour Your love into me so that it overflows to others and glorifies You in the process.

I will bless the LORD at all times; His praise shall continually be in my mouth. My soul shall make its boast in the LORD; the humble shall hear of it and be glad.

PSALM 34:1-2

PRAYER NOTES

_____

_____

_____

_____

_____

_____

Make Worship a Habit

LORD, You have saved me and given me a foundation that is unshakable. "You enlarged my path under me, so my feet did not slip" (2 Samuel 22:37). It is my greatest privilege to exalt You above all and proclaim that You are King of kings and Lord of lords. I praise You for Your Holy Spirit, who leads and comforts me. I praise You for your wisdom and revelation. I praise You for Your peace and joy. Thank You that You are in charge of my life and nothing is too hard for You. Thank You for enabling me to do what I could never *do* without you. Lord, help me to worship You in ways that are pleasing in Your sight.

*The hour is coming, and now is, when
the true worshipers will worship the
Father in spirit and truth; for the Father
is seeking such to worship Him.*

JOHN 4:23

PRAYER NOTES

_____

_____

_____

_____

_____

Pray As Though Your Life Depends on It

⸻⸻

LORD, teach me to pray. Help me to pray about not just *my* needs, but also the needs of others. Show me how to pray about everything. I cry out to You and declare my trouble before You (Psalm 142:1-2). Enable me to "pray without ceasing" (1 Thessalonians 5:17). Help me to leave the things I pray about at Your feet and in Your hands. Teach me to trust You so much that I don't have preconceived ideas about the way my prayers must be answered. I know it is my job to pray and Your job to answer. Help me to do my job and let You do Yours. Help me to trust that You will answer in Your way and in Your time.

*Whatever things you ask in prayer,
believing, you will receive.*

MATTHEW 21:22

PRAYER NOTES

Pray As Though Your Life Depends on It

LORD, I know Your judgments are perfect, and so I will praise You above all things—even my own desires and expectations. You are my Resting Place and the Solid Rock on which I stand. Nothing will shake me, not even seemingly unanswered prayers. When I can't see the answers to my prayers, open my eyes to see things from Your perspective. "I will lift up my eyes to the hills—from whence comes my help? My help comes from the LORD, who made heaven and earth" (Psalm 121:1-2). I am grateful that You, who are the all-powerful, all-knowing God of the universe, are also my heavenly Father, who loves me unconditionally and will never forsake me. Thank You for hearing and answering my prayers.

Continue earnestly in prayer, being vigilant in it with thanksgiving.

Colossians 4:2

Prayer Notes

Live in the Freedom God Has for You

————

LORD, I thank You that You are "my fortress, my high tower and my deliverer, my shield and the One in whom I take refuge" (Psalm 144:2). Thank You that "You have delivered my soul from death," and have "kept my feet from falling," so that I may walk before You (Psalm 56:13). Show me anything I need to be set free from. I don't want to be living with something from which You already paid the price for me to be liberated. I pray that You "will deliver me from every evil work and preserve me" for Your kingdom (2 Timothy 4:18). "O God, do not be far from me; O my God, make haste to help me!" (Psalm 71:12).

You are my hiding place; You shall preserve
me from trouble; You shall surround
me with songs of deliverance.

PSALM 32:7

PRAYER NOTES

Live in the Freedom God Has for You

LORD, I see that the forces rising up against Your believers are powerful, but I know You are far more powerful than they are. Reveal to my heart Your power and might. "You *are* my help and my deliverer; do not delay, O my God" (Psalm 40:17). I cry out to You to liberate me from the enemy who tries to put me into bondage. I thank You that You will answer by setting me free (Psalm 118:5). Thank You that You will never give up on me but will continue to deliver me (2 Corinthians 1:9-10). Thank You, Lord, that You will deliver me from all evil and be with me in trouble. To You "be glory forever and ever" (2 Timothy 4:18).

He shall call upon Me, and I will answer him;
I will be with him in trouble; I will deliver
him and honor him. With long life I will
satisfy him, and show him My salvation.

PSALM 91:15-16

PRAYER NOTES

Seek God's Kingdom and His Gifts

LORD, I come humbly before You and seek Your kingdom and Your dominion in my heart and life above all else. May Your kingdom be established wherever I go and in whatever I do. Make me a pure vessel for Your power to go forth and proclaim the rule of King Jesus where You have given me influence and opportunity to do so. Thank You, Lord, for Your many gifts to me. Thank You for Your gifts of salvation, justification, righteousness, eternal life, and grace. Thank You for Your gifts of love, peace, and joy. Thank You that these will never fail in my life because You are my everlasting Father and *You* will never fail.

*Do not fear, little flock, for it is your Father's
good pleasure to give you the kingdom.*

LUKE 12:32

PRAYER NOTES

_____

_____

_____

_____

_____

_____

Seek God's Kingdom and His Gifts

———

LORD, Your unfailing love is a great comfort to me (Psalm 119:76 NIV). Thank You that nothing can ever separate me from Your love (Romans 8:35-39). Thank You for Your grace that gives me far better than I deserve. Thank You, Jesus, for taking the consequences of my sin. Thank You for giving me the mind of Christ and Your wisdom and knowledge of the truth. I pray You will teach me all the "mysteries of the kingdom of heaven" (Matthew 13:11). Help me to seek Your kingdom every day and to live in the gifts You have given me. "For Yours is the kingdom and the power and the glory forever" (Matthew 6:13).

*To each one of us grace was given according
to the measure of Christ's gift.*

Ephesians 4:7

Prayer Notes

Maintain a Right Heart

———

LORD, create in me a clean heart. Set me free from anything that is not of You. Cleanse my heart of all sin, and direct it to Your ways (Psalm 119:36). Help me to hide Your Word in my heart so that I will not sin against You (Psalm 119:11). Keep me always awed by Your Word (Psalm 119:161). I don't want any sin in my heart to hinder my prayers to You (Psalm 66:18). Keep me undeceived (Deuteronomy 11:16). Help me not to foolishly trust my own heart, but instead to trust You to reveal the truth I need to see (Proverbs 28:26). Give me a wise heart so that I can receive all Your commands (Proverbs 10:8).

Keep your heart with all diligence,
for out of it spring the issues of life.

PROVERBS 4:23

PRAYER NOTES

Maintain a Right Heart

HOLY SPIRIT, align my heart with Yours. Flush out of my heart all that is dark and wrong and replace it with more of You. Search my heart and make changes wherever they are needed. Soften my heart where it has become hard. Purify my heart where it has become polluted. Help me to set nothing wicked before my eyes. Lord, I pray that You would take away anything in my heart that keeps me from being a full partaker of Your holiness (Hebrews 12:10). Help me to praise You with my whole heart, so that I withhold nothing from You (Psalm 9:1). Teach me to always maintain a right heart before You.

*Blessed are the pure in heart,
for they shall see God.*

MATTHEW 5:8

PRAYER NOTES

Move in Forgiveness— God's and Yours

LORD, I thank You for forgiving me and not even remembering my sins anymore (Hebrews 8:12). Show me anything I need to confess to You today so that I can bring it before You and be set free. I especially ask that You would reveal any place in my heart where I have not forgiven someone. I don't want to harbor anything within me that will keep my prayers from being heard. I don't want to live in unforgiveness anymore, for any reason. Help me to be a forgiving person in the same way You are forgiving toward me. Help me to always forgive quickly and not wait for the other person to say or do what I think they should.

*Be kind to one another, tenderhearted,
forgiving one another, even as
God in Christ forgave you.*

EPHESIANS 4:32

PRAYER NOTES

_____

_____

_____

_____

_____

_____

Move in Forgiveness— God's and Yours

LORD, show me any way I need to ask someone to forgive me so that we both can be healed and set free. If I have hurt someone without realizing it and unforgiveness is in his (her) heart, reveal that to me so I can make amends. If I have been selfish, and that has diminished the way someone feels about himself (herself), enable me to clear the air between us. Lord, take away anything of anger, bitterness, or resentment in my heart. Pour out Your Spirit upon me and cleanse me of all that is not of You. Enable me to be a person who lives in the forgiveness You have given me so I can extend forgiveness freely toward others (Ephesians 4:32).

Judge not, and you shall not be judged.
Condemn not, and you shall not be condemned.
Forgive, and you will be forgiven.

LUKE 6:37

PRAYER NOTES

Fear God, but Don't Live in Fear

LORD, I bring all my fears to You and ask You to take them from me so that I no longer live in fear of anything. You are "my light and my salvation" and "the strength of my life. Of whom shall I be afraid?" (Psalm 27:1). I know You have not given me a spirit of fear; You have given me love, power, and a sound mind. In Your presence all my fear is gone, for Your love takes it away. Help me to give the glory due You at all times, for I worship and praise You above all else. Enlarge my faith to extinguish all fear, so that I trust in Your Word and Your power to protect me.

*As a father has compassion on
his children, so the LORD has
compassion on those who fear him.*

PSALM 103:13 NIV

PRAYER NOTES

_____

_____

_____

_____

_____

_____

Fear God, but Don't Live in Fear

LORD, Your Word says "though an army may encamp against me, my heart shall not fear" (Psalm 27:3). How grateful I am that when I cry out to You, You hear me and deliver me from all my fears (Psalm 34:4). I know reverence of You brings life and keeps me away from the pitfalls that lead to death (Proverb 14:27). Enable me to have that godly fear in my heart always. I don't want to sacrifice any of the blessings, protection, wisdom, fulfillment, peace, and long life You have for those who fear You. Help me to make praise my first reaction to fear whenever it comes upon me. I don't want to deny Your presence by giving place to fear in times of weakness.

*The fear of the LORD is a fountain of life,
to turn one away from the snares of death.*

PROVERBS 14:27

PRAYER NOTES

_____

_____

_____

_____

_____

_____

Replace Doubt with Unwavering Faith

JESUS, You are "the author and finisher" of my faith (Hebrews 12:2). Thank You for the gift of faith You have given me. Increase my faith every day as I read Your Word. Give me strong faith to believe for the answers to my prayers. I know that it is not about me trying to establish great faith on my own, but that faith comes from Your Spirit and Your Word. I know that "whatever is not from faith is sin," so I confess all doubt within me (Romans 14:23). Your Word says that anyone who doubts is unstable and double-minded and cannot please You (James 1:6-8). I pray You will make me to be strong in faith that pleases You.

Without faith it is impossible to please Him, for he who comes to God must believe that He is, and that He is a rewarder of those who diligently seek Him.

HEBREWS 11:6

PRAYER NOTES

24

Replace Doubt with Unwavering Faith

5-25-22

LORD, You are everything to me. I know that because of You I am never without love, joy, hope, power, protection, and provision. Because of You I can rise above my limitations and live in peace, knowing You will work things out for my good as I live Your way. Help me to read Your Word every day. Open my eyes more and more to Your truth. Enable me to recognize and understand Your promises to me so that I can daily choose to reject all doubt in my life. I acknowledge You in all my ways and depend on You to direct my path (Proverbs 3:5-6). Help me to trust You in all things every day. Keep me from doubting You and Your Word.

*I have been crucified with Christ; it is no
longer I who live, but Christ lives in me;
and the life I live which I now live in the
flesh I live by faith in the Son of God, who
loved me and gave Himself for me.*

GALATIANS 2:20

PRAYER NOTES

_____

_____

_____

_____

_____

_____

25

Welcome God's Will and Do It

LORD, I pray You would teach me to do Your will (Psalm 143:10). Work the desire for Your will into my heart (Philippians 2:13). Help me to "stand perfect and complete" in Your will and stay in the center of it at all times (Colossian 4:12). I am grateful to You that Your will can be known. Guide my every step so that I don't make a wrong decision or take a wrong path. "I delight to do Your will, O my God" (Psalm 40:8). Fill me with the knowledge of Your will in all wisdom and spiritual understanding (Colossians 1:9). Line the desires of my heart up with the desires of Your heart. I want what You want for my life.

*This is the confidence that we have
in Him, that if we ask anything
according to His will, He hears us.*

1 John 5:14

PRAYER NOTES

_____

_____

_____

_____

_____

_____

_____

26

Welcome God's Will and Do It

LORD, help me to refuse to hold on to things that are not of You. Help me to cling to You instead of my own dreams. I only want to do Your will from my whole heart (Ephesians 6:6). When I experience difficult times, help me to know if it is because I have done something wrong, or if it is that I have done something right and this is happening according to Your will (1 Peter 4:19). Lord, only You know what is right for me. Help me to hear Your voice leading me. Transform me to do Your will (Romans 12:2). Help me to have endurance so that I can do Your perfect will and receive the promises of all You have for me.

May the God of peace…make you complete in every good work to do His will, working in you what is well pleasing in His sight, through Jesus Christ, to whom be glory forever and ever.

HEBREWS 13:20-21

PRAYER NOTES

_____

_____

_____

_____

_____

_____

27

Recognize Your Purpose and Work to Fulfill It

LORD, You knew me before I was born. Thank You that You predestined me to be saved and conformed to the image of Jesus. Thank You that You have called me and prepared me to glorify You (Romans 8:29-30). Give me a clear sense of Your purpose in my life. Help me to understand what is the hope of my calling and the exceeding greatness of Your power to enable me to fulfill that purpose. May everything I do support Your plans for my life. Show me the gifts You have put in me and how I can best develop them and use them for Your pleasure. Help me to live every day with a deep sense of Your purpose in my life.

We know that all things work together for good to those who love God, to those who are the called according to His purpose.

ROMANS 8:28

PRAYER NOTES

28

Recognize Your Purpose and Work to Fulfill It

LORD, I commit my work to You. I pray that I will always be in Your will in whatever I do, and that I will do it well. I pray that all I do is pleasing to You and to those for whom and with whom I am working. Establish the work of my hands for Your pleasure and Your glory (Psalm 90:17). Help me to understand what is the hope of my calling (Ephesians 1:17-18). Enable me to "be steadfast, immovable, always abounding in the work of the Lord" that You have given me to do, knowing that my "labor is not in vain in the Lord"—as long as it is *from* You and *for* You (1 Corinthians 15:58).

May He grant you according to your heart's desire, and fulfill all your purpose.

Psalm 20:4

PRAYER NOTES

29

Bask in God's Love

LORD, I thank You that You are the God of love. Thank You for loving me even before I knew You (Romans 5:8). Thank You for sending Your Son, Jesus, to die for me and take on Himself all I deserve. Thank You, Jesus, that You have given me life with You forever, and a better life now. Your love heals me and makes me whole. "You are my Lord, my goodness is nothing apart from You" (Psalm 16:2). I know there is a great dimension of healing and wholeness that can only happen in the presence of Your love. Enable me to open up to Your love working in my life like never before. Wash over me with Your love today.

Beloved, let us love one another, for love is of God; and everyone who loves is born of God and knows God. He who does not love does not know God, for God is love.

1 JOHN 4:7-8

PRAYER NOTES

30

Bask in God's Love

LORD, fill my heart with Your love in greater measure so I can be the whole person You created me to be. Give me Your heart of love for others. I pray I will be so filled with Your love that it overflows to other people in a way they can perceive it. Show me the loving thing to do in every situation. How grateful I am that nothing can separate me from Your love, no matter where I go or what I do—not even my own failings (Romans 8:35-39). Thank You that because of Your love for me, I am more than a conqueror (Romans 8:37). Thank You, Lord, that Your unfailing love and mercy surround me because I trust in You (Psalm 32:10).

I am persuaded that neither death nor life, nor angels nor principalities nor powers, nor things present nor things to come, nor height nor depth, nor any other created thing, shall be able to separate us from the love of God which is in Christ Jesus our Lord.

ROMANS 8:38-39

PRAYER NOTES

31

Put Your Hope in the Lord

LORD, in You I put all my hope and expectations. "I will hope continually, and will praise You yet more and more" (Psalm 71:14). I know I have no hope without You (Ephesians 2:12), so my hope is entirely in You (Psalm 39:7). "For You are my hope, O Lord GOD; You are my trust from my youth" (Psalm 71:5). In the times I am tempted to feel hopeless—especially when I don't see answers to my prayers for a long time and I become discouraged—help me to put my eyes back on You. Enable me to end all feelings of hopelessness in my life. Help me to see they are not true and that only Your Word is true.

May the God of hope fill you with all joy and peace in believing, that you may abound in hope by the power of the Holy Spirit.

ROMANS 15:13

PRAYER NOTES

_____

_____

_____

_____

_____

_____

32

Put Your Hope in the Lord

———

LORD, when I pray for a person or a situation and don't see changes, help me to not put my hope in answered prayer, but rather to put my hope in You, the One who answers my prayers. Where I have put my hope and expectations on people or circumstances, I confess that as a lack of faith in You and Your Word. I take comfort in Your Word and Your promises. I trust in You—the God of hope—who has given me every reason to hope. Help me to see that having hope is a big issue, and that it is a clear indicator of the condition of my heart. In Your presence is where my heart has found a home.

Hope does not disappoint, because the love of God has been poured out in our hearts by the Holy Spirit who was given to us.

ROMANS 5:5

PRAYER NOTES

33

Give God's Way—
to Him and to Others

LORD, teach me how to give to You with a cheerful attitude. Help me to be diligent in this step of obedience. I don't ever want to rob You; I want only to bless You. Help me to give to You as You require. Teach my heart to release back to You all You have given to me. Help me to reject the fear of not having enough. When I become fearful, help me to put my trust in You. You are greater than any lack I may face. Help me to have a "generous soul" and a "generous eye" (Proverbs 11:25; 22:9). Show me specific ways I can give to others. Reveal their needs to me and how I can meet them.

The generous soul will be made rich, and he who waters will also be watered himself.

PROVERBS 11:25

PRAYER NOTES

_____

_____

_____

_____

_____

_____

34

Give God's Way—
to Him and to Others

—————

LORD, I don't want to stop up the flow of Your blessings in my life by not giving when and where I should. I am grateful for all You have given me, but I pray I will not merely give to get, but give only to please You. Help me to understand the release that happens in my life when I give, so that I can let go of things. Help me to "not forget to do good and to share," for I know that with such sacrifices, You are "well pleased" (Hebrews 13:16). Help me to give and thereby store up treasures in heaven that do not fail, for I know that where my treasure is, my heart will be there also (Luke 12:33-34).

Blessed is he who considers the poor; the
LORD will deliver him in time of trouble.
The LORD will preserve him and keep him
alive, and he will be blessed on the earth.

PSALM 41:1-2

PRAYER NOTES

_____

_____

_____

_____

_____

_____

35

Take Control of Your Thoughts

LORD, help me to cast down every thought I have that is not glorifying to You. Enable me to bring my thoughts into captivity and obedience to You and Your ways. I know it is "You who test the righteous, and see the mind and heart" (Jeremiah 20:12). Show me what is in my mind and heart that is not pleasing to You. "Examine me, O LORD, and prove me; try my mind and my heart" (Psalm 26:2). Help me to live each day with the love, power, and sound mind You have given me. Give me clarity of thought to replace any confusion. I pray that Your Word will discern my "thoughts and intents of the heart" whenever I read it (Hebrews 4:12).

Do not be conformed to this world, but be transformed by the renewing of your mind, that you may prove what is that good and acceptable and perfect will of God.

ROMANS 12:2

PRAYER NOTES

_____

_____

_____

_____

_____

36

Take Control of Your Thoughts

LORD, teach me the truth of Your Word so well that I recognize a lie the moment it presents itself. I know I cannot move into all You have for me if I believe lies about myself, my circumstances, or You. Help me to silence the voice of the enemy by speaking Your truth. Enable me to choose this day to fill my mind with "the best, not the worst; the beautiful, not the ugly; things to praise, not things to curse" (Philippians 4:8 MSG). Help me to not entertain thoughts of unforgiveness against anyone, nor dwell on what has happened in the past. I pray that Your peace, which surpasses all understanding, will guard my heart and mind through Jesus, my Lord (Philippians 4:7).

You will keep him in perfect peace,
whose mind is stayed on You,
because he trusts in You.

Isaiah 26:3

Prayer Notes

_____

_____

_____

_____

_____

_____

37

Refuse Negative Emotions

LORD, today I refuse all depression, anxiety, fear, dread, anger, and sadness, for I know they are not from You. By the power of Your Holy Spirit I resist the temptation to see the bad in life, and I ask You to open my eyes to the good. Enable me to sense Your presence at all times, no matter what is happening. My life is in Your hands, and Your love sustains me. May Your joy rise in my heart so fully that it crowds out all that is not of You. I pray that You would evaporate any heaviness in me. Enable me to breathe the fresh air of Your Spirit blowing the dark clouds away. Thank You that You are my light.

The LORD redeems the soul of His servants, and none of those who trust in Him shall be condemned.

PSALM 34:22

PRAYER NOTES

_____

_____

_____

_____

_____

_____

38

Refuse Negative Emotions

LORD, help me to see anything I dread as a challenge that I can rise above, because You enable me. You have brought me out of darkness and the shadow of death, and broken my chains of bondage (Psalm 107:14). You have delivered me from darkness and brought me into Your kingdom and Your love (Colossians 1:13). Because You are my salvation, I don't have to be afraid (Psalm 27:1). I can call to You and You will save me (Psalm 107:13). Help me to worship You often. Set me free from all negative emotions that have become a habit. Give me a garment of praise to take away the spirit of heaviness. In Your presence I find fullness of joy (Psalm 16:11).

In the day when I cried out, You answered me,
and made me bold with strength in my soul.

PSALM 138:3

PRAYER NOTES

_____

_____

_____

_____

_____

_____

39

Treat Your Body As Though It Belongs to God

LORD, I commit my body to You as the temple of Your Holy Spirit. Teach me how to care for it properly. Show me how I should eat and what I should avoid. Take away all desire for food that is harmful to me. Give me balance and wisdom. Help me to purify myself from everything that contaminates my body and spirit out of reverence for You (2 Corinthians 7:1). Enable me to live Your way so that I can dwell in the peace You have for me. Show me where I allow unnecessary stress to rule in my life, and help me to take steps to alleviate it. Teach me to simplify my life, so that I can live better and healthier.

*Whether you eat or drink or whatever
you do, do it all for the glory of God.*

1 Corinthians 10:31 niv

Prayer Notes

40

Treat Your Body As Though It Belongs to God

———

LORD, help me to rest at night, as You created me to do, "for I know that a heart at peace gives life to the body" (Proverbs 14:30 NIV). Help me to exercise as I should so that my body stays strong. Where I have long-entrenched bad habits when it comes to proper care for my body, I ask You to reveal them all to me and enable me take the necessary steps to get free. Help me to love and appreciate my body and not be critical of it. Enable me to choose life (Deuteronomy 30:19). Even though my flesh and heart may fail, You are the strength of my heart forever (Psalm 73:26). Enable me to go from "strength to strength" (Psalm 84:7).

*Therefore, I urge you, brothers, in view of
God's mercy, to offer your bodies as living
sacrifices, holy and pleasing to God—
this is your spiritual act of worship.*

ROMANS 12:1 NIV

PRAYER NOTES

_____

_____

_____

_____

_____

_____

41

Trust in Your Healer

LORD, thank You for Your healing power on my behalf. Thank You for sending forth Your Word to heal me (Psalm 107:20). I believe You, Jesus, are the living Word. You paid the price on the cross to purchase healing for me. You took my infirmities and bore my sickness. There is healing in Your name, and I believe You are my Healer. Thank You for Your written Word, which comes alive in my heart as I read it, speak it, or hear it. I pray Your Word in my heart will be medicine for my body. I praise You, Lord, for all Your promises of safety, protection, and healing. I choose to believe Your Word and have faith in You and Your power to heal.

Heal me, O LORD, and I shall be healed; save me, and I shall be saved, for You are my praise.

JEREMIAH 17:14

PRAYER NOTES

42

Trust in Your Healer

———

LORD, restore health to me and heal me of all my wounds (Jeremiah 30:17). Enlarge my faith in You and Your name so that I can lay hold of the healing You paid for on the cross. Help me not to give up praying until I see the healing You have for me. I know that when You heal me, I am truly healed (Jeremiah 17:14). Teach me how to pray in power and faith for the healing of others. Every time I pray for someone else, hear my prayer and answer by touching that person with Your healing power. Show me how to pray so that You can do a miracle, not only in my life but also in the lives of other people.

Surely He has borne our griefs and carried our sorrows; yet we esteemed Him stricken, smitten by God, and afflicted. But He was wounded for our transgressions, He was bruised for our iniquities; the chastisement for our peace was upon Him, and by His stripes we are healed.

ISAIAH 53:4-5

PRAYER NOTES

43

Say "No Way" to Temptation

LORD, I pray You would lead me far away from all temptation to do or think anything that is not pleasing to You. Help me to always know what is right and enable me to do it. Deliver me from all attacks of the evil one, who tries to entice me away from what is good in Your sight. I pray that the weakness of my flesh will be overcome by the strength and power of Your Spirit. I choose to be God controlled and not flesh controlled. I know that I am dead to sin but alive in Christ Jesus, and therefore I will not allow sin to reign in me. Help me to know Your Word well and remember it at all times.

Be sober, be vigilant; because your adversary the devil walks about like a roaring lion, seeking whom he may devour. Resist him, steadfast in the faith, knowing that the same sufferings are experienced by your brotherhood in the world.

1 Peter 5:8-9

PRAYER NOTES

_____

_____

_____

_____

_____

_____

44

Say "No Way" to Temptation

LORD, I declare that sin will not have dominion over me, for by Your power and grace I can resist it (Romans 6:11-14). I know I can't stand strong if I don't stand on the truth of Your Word. Lord, I thank You that You will not allow me to be tempted beyond what I am able to handle. Thank You for making a way for me to escape temptation (1 Corinthians 10:13). I turn to You, Lord, and ask that by the power of Your Holy Spirit You will help me to withstand any onslaught of the enemy. Teach me to take up "the shield of faith," with which I will be able to "quench all the fiery darts of the wicked one" (Ephesians 6:16).

No temptation has overtaken you except such as is common to man; but God is faithful, who will not allow you to be tempted beyond what you are able, but with the temptation will also make the way of escape, that you may be able to bear it.

1 Corinthians 10:13

PRAYER NOTES

45

Step Out of Destructive Relationships

———

LORD, I thank You for the people You have put into my life. Make all my good relationships stronger. Help me to handle the difficult ones in a way that pleases You. Remove any hopelessly destructive relationship from my life by either changing it for the better or by helping me to walk away from it. Give me wisdom about the friends I choose. Help me not to ever be in a relationship with anyone who will lead me off the path You have for me. If there is any relationship I have that is destructive for either of us, enable us both to change in order to make it better or help us to let it go. Teach me to be a good friend to others.

*Two are better than one, because they have
a good reward for their labor. For if they
fall, one will lift up his companion.*

ECCLESIASTES 4:9-10

PRAYER NOTES

46

Step Out of
Destructive Relationships

LORD, I pray You would send people into my life who are godly, wise, and strong in their knowledge of You. Help us to contribute to the quality of each other's lives. Help me to always exhibit Your love to others. Enable me to love others as myself (Galatians 5:14). Remind me to always be quick to forgive in any relationship. Show me the relationships that are worth fighting for, and help me to see when a relationship will always be destructive no matter what I do. Enable me to move with the leading of Your Holy Spirit in this. I ask You to be in charge of all of my relationships so that they will be what You want them to be.

Through love serve one another. For all the law is fulfilled in one word, even in this: "You shall love your neighbor as yourself."

GALATIANS 5:13-14

PRAYER NOTES

_____

_____

_____

_____

_____

_____

_____

47

Speak Words That Bring Life

GOD, help me to speak words that lift up and not tear down, words that compliment instead of criticize, words that speak unconditional love and not human expectations, and words that instill confidence and not uneasiness. Help me to have such faith in Your control in my life that I can "do all things without complaining and disputing" (Philippians 2:14). Where I have said words that are negative about myself or anyone else, forgive me. I want to be kind with my words and to daily remember that "the tongue of the wise promotes health" (Proverbs 12:18). Fill me afresh with Your Holy Spirit and pour into my heart Your love, peace, and joy. Help me to treat myself and others with respect, patience, and love.

The Lord GOD has given Me the tongue of the learned, that I should know how to speak a word in season to him who is weary.

Isaiah 50:4

PRAYER NOTES

_____

_____

_____

_____

_____

_____

_____

48

Speak Words That Bring Life

LORD, help me to always say with conviction that I will not sin with my mouth (Psalm 17:3). Help me refuse to say negative things about myself. Every time I start to say a critical word, help me to stop immediately and not continue that line of thinking. Teach me to monitor the words I speak to others. Keep me from saying wrong words that may hurt someone or diminish them in any way. Help me not to be careless in this regard. Teach me to always speak words that are supported by Your truth and glorify You. "Let the words of my mouth and the meditation of my heart be acceptable in Your sight, O LORD, my strength and my Redeemer" (Psalm 19:14).

I have put My words in your mouth; I have covered you with the shadow of My hand.

ISAIAH 51:16

PRAYER NOTES

_____

_____

_____

_____

_____

_____

49

Be Holy as God Is Holy

LORD, help me to be holy as You are holy. Jesus, help me to walk as You walked on earth (1 John 2:6). Enable me to be an imitator of You (Ephesians 5:1). Wash over me with Your holiness and cleanse me from the inside out of anything in me that is not holy. Reveal whatever is hidden within me that I need to be rid of—any attitudes, thoughts, or sin that must be gone from my life. Separate me from all that separates me from You, Lord. Help me to get rid of anything in my life that does not glorify You. Give me the conviction and strength I need to step away from whatever is not compatible with Your holiness in me.

We, being delivered from the hand of our enemies,
might serve Him without fear, in holiness and
righteousness before Him all the days of our life.

LUKE 1:74-75

PRAYER NOTES

_____

_____

_____

_____

_____

_____

50

Be Holy as God Is Holy

LORD, "who is like You, glorious in holiness"?
(Exodus 15:11). You are mighty and have done
great things for me. Holy is Your name (Luke
1:49). Help me to continually maintain a humble
heart of worship before You. Purify my heart and
mind so that I can be a partaker of Your holiness
(Hebrews 12:10). You are worthy of all praise and
honor and glory, for only You are holy. "O LORD,
You are my God. I will exalt You, I will praise
Your name, for You have done wonderful things"
(Isaiah 25:1). I sing praise to You, Lord, and give
thanks at the remembrance of Your holy name
(Psalm 30:4). I worship You in the beauty of Your
holiness (Psalm 29:2).

*He chose us in Him before the foundation
of the world, that we should be holy and
without blame before Him in love.*

Ephesians 1:4

Prayer Notes

51

Recognize Your Enemy

LORD, I thank You that You have delivered me from my enemy. Thank You, Jesus, that You came to "destroy the works of the devil" and You have already won the battle (1 John 3:8). I know that "though I walk in the midst of trouble, You will revive me; You will stretch out Your hand against the wrath of my enemies, and Your right hand will save me" (Psalm 138:7). Help me to "be wise in what is good, and simple concerning evil" for I know that You, the God of peace, "will crush Satan" under my feet quickly (Romans 16:19-20). Help me to "take up the whole armor of God," so that I can stand strong during enemy attack (Ephesians 6:13).

He preserves the souls of His saints; He delivers them out of the hand of the wicked.

PSALM 97:10

PRAYER NOTES

_____

_____

_____

_____

_____

_____

52

Recognize Your Enemy

LORD, keep me aware of when the enemy is attacking. Help me to be strong in Your Word and continuously in prayer so that I will not be caught off guard. Help me to never "give place to the devil" with disobedience to Your ways (Ephesians 4:27). Help me instead to submit to You and resist the devil so that he will flee from me (James 4:7). Enable me to stay in Your will so that I never come out from under the umbrella of Your protection. Teach me to make worship of You my first reaction to enemy attack. I praise You, Lord, for You have "delivered me out of all trouble; and my eye has seen its desire upon my enemies" (Psalm 54:7).

Let the redeemed of the LORD say so, whom He has redeemed from the hand of the enemy.

PSALM 107:2

PRAYER NOTES

_____

_____

_____

_____

_____

_____

_____

53

Fast and Pray to Win

LORD, help me to fast and pray to Your glory. Enable me to put aside one of my favorite activities—eating the food You have provided for me—in favor of exalting You as everything in my life. Show me how often and how long I should fast, and enable me to accomplish it. Help me to be well enough and strong enough to fast in the way You want me to. Thank You that when I fast, You will break down the strongholds of the enemy in my life and loose all bonds of wickedness. I pray You will break any wrong thinking in me. Release me from the heavy burdens I have been carrying. Break every yoke of bondage in my life.

*When you fast, anoint your head and wash
your face, so that you do not appear to men
to be fasting, but to your Father who is
in the secret place; and your Father who
sees in secret will reward you openly.*

MATTHEW 6:17-18

PRAYER NOTES

_____

_____

_____

_____

_____

_____

54

Fast and Pray to Win

LORD, reveal ways to pray I don't yet understand as I fast. Help me to do what I can to help others and feed the hungry. Show me where I should extend myself to those who are afflicted or suffering. Help me to honor the Sabbath—Your holy day—by doing what honors You and not going my own way and doing what I want. Help me to want what *You* want. Thank You that as I fast, You will look after the details of my life and give me direction. Thank You that my "light shall break forth like the morning" and my "healing shall spring forth speedily" (Isaiah 58:8). Thank You that when I call, You will answer (Isaiah 58:9).

Is this not the fast that I have chosen: to loose the bonds of wickedness, to undo the heavy burdens, to let the oppressed go free, and that you break every yoke?

Isaiah 58:6

PRAYER NOTES

_____

_____

_____

_____

_____

_____

55

Stand Strong in Tough Times

LORD, I pray You would help me to stand strong in all I know of You. Teach me to stand on Your Word, no matter what is happening in my life. Enable me to be obedient to Your ways. I acknowledge that I am weak, but I rejoice that You are strong in me—especially during times of trial and difficulty. Help me to learn what I need to know from each challenge I face. Lead me on the path You have for me. I don't want to take a single step without You. Help me in the situation I am facing now. Lift me out of any hopelessness, fear, doubt, or frustration. Enable me to be firm in faith and always abiding in Your will.

He said to me, "My grace is sufficient for you, for My strength is made perfect in weakness." Therefore most gladly I will rather boast in my infirmities, that the power of Christ may rest upon me.

2 CORINTHIANS 12:9

PRAYER NOTES

_____

_____

_____

_____

_____

_____

56

Stand Strong in Tough Times

———

LORD, thank You for helping me stand strong. You have armed me with strength for the battle (Psalm 18:39). So many times "I would have lost heart, unless I had believed that I would see the goodness of the LORD in the land of the living" (Psalm 27:13). Help me to become so strong in You that I can stand without wavering, no matter what happens. Teach me to rest in You, knowing that You will give me what I need for the moment I am in. I am determined to "count it all joy" when I go through trials, because of the perfecting work You will do for me (James 1:2-4). "Though I walk in the midst of trouble, You will revive me" (Psalm 138:7).

My brethren, count it all joy when you fall into various trials, knowing that the testing of your faith produces patience. But let patience have its perfect work, that you may be perfect and complete, lacking nothing.

JAMES 1:2-4

PRAYER NOTES

57

Move in the Power of God

LORD, I am grateful for Your power extended to me. You have shown Yourself strong on my behalf countless times because my heart is loyal to You (2 Chronicles 16:9). By Your great and almighty power You have saved and redeemed me (Nehemiah 1:10). You have delivered me, protected me, and provided for me, and I know You will continue to do so. You uphold all things by the word of Your power (Hebrews 1:3). Thank You that because You are all-powerful, that means all things are possible. Therefore I refuse to become discouraged or fearful about any aspect of my life. I will not trust in the wisdom of man, but I will trust in You and Your perfect wisdom and power.

The eyes of the LORD run to and fro throughout the whole earth, to show Himself strong on behalf of those whose heart is loyal to Him.

2 CHRONICLES 16:9

PRAYER NOTES

58

Move in the Power of God

LORD, You give power to the weak and increase their strength (Isaiah 40:29). I thank You that I am the beneficiary of that. Help me to never forget Your power to redeem, save, restore, and renew. No matter what happens, I want to turn to You first and move in the power of Your Spirit. "Be exalted, O LORD, in Your own strength!" I will "sing and praise Your power" (Psalm 21:13). All power belongs to You, Lord (Psalm 62:11). God of hope, help me to "abound in hope by the power of the Holy Spirit" (Romans 15:13). Thank You for the exceeding greatness of Your power toward those who believe (Ephesians 1:19). "For Yours is the power and the glory forever" (Matthew 6:13).

Yours, O LORD, is the greatness, the power and the glory, the victory and the majesty; for all that is in heaven and in earth is Yours.

1 CHRONICLES 29:11

PRAYER NOTES

_____

_____

_____

_____

_____

_____

_____

59

Refuse to Give Up

LORD, my hope is in You, and I know You will never fail me. Thank You that Your restoration is ongoing in my life. I am grateful that I am Your child and You have given me a purpose. Thank You for the great future You have for me because You love me (1 Corinthians 2:9). Thank You that I am complete in You (Colossians 2:10). Thank You that I am never alone (Matthew 28:20). Help me to not think of giving up when things become difficult. Help me to remember that even in hard times You will help me persevere. Keep me from becoming discouraged in times of waiting. I know Your timing is perfect and the way You do things is right.

I will bless the LORD who has given me counsel;
my heart also instructs me in the night seasons.
I have set the LORD always before me; because
He is at my right hand I shall not be moved.

PSALM 16:7-8

PRAYER NOTES

60

Refuse to Give Up

———

LORD, help me to cling to Your promises so that they are engraved upon my heart and are alive within me. Enable me to "not remember the former things, nor consider the things of old" (Isaiah 43:18). I know You are doing a new thing in me. I pray it will "spring forth" speedily. I pray You will "make a road in the wilderness and rivers in the desert" for me (Isaiah 43:18-19). I know I'm often in a hurry for things to happen, and I ask You to forgive me when I have tried to put You on my schedule. I pray that by patience I will possess my soul (Luke 21:19). Thank You that You "will perfect that which concerns me" (Psalm 138:8).

"For the mountains shall depart and the hills be removed, but My kindness shall not depart from you, nor shall My covenant of peace be removed," says the LORD, who has mercy on you.

ISAIAH 54:10

PRAYER NOTES

Other Books
by Stormie Omartian

Lead Me, Holy Spirit
In this life-changing book, Stormie looks at the Holy Spirit and how He wants those who know Him to hear when He speaks to their heart, soul, and spirit. Of how He wants to help believers enter into the relationship with God they yearn for, the wholeness and freedom God has for them, and the fulfillment of God's promises to them.

Just Enough Light for the Step I'm On
All Christians, especially those experiencing life changes or difficult times, will appreciate Stormie's honesty, candor, and advice, based on experience and the Word of God, as she show readers how to walk in peace through the pressures of today's world.

The Prayer That Changes Everything®
Stormie's warm, personal stories, biblical truths, and practical guiding principles reveal the changes to circumstances that can take place when Christians praise God during times of difficulty, sorrow, and fear as well as abundance and joy.

The Power of Prayer™ to Change Your Marriage
Stormie gives 14 ways to meet the 14 challenges to every marriage so that your marriage can last a lifetime. This is the follow-up book to her bestselling books *The Power of a Praying® Wife* and *The Power of a Praying® Husband.*

The Power of Praying® for Your Adult Children
For more than 15 years, millions of parents have prayed for their children using Stormie's book *The Power of a Praying® Parent.* As children become adults, they need prayer just as much, and Stormie has provided new, helpful, and effective ways for every parent to pray and find peace in the process.